HOW I KNOW THE SKY IS A RIVER

selected and new shorter poems 1978–1998

Allan Safarik

The publishers gratefully acknowledge the support of the Saskatchewan Arts Board in the publication of this book.

Edited by John Livingstone Clark
Cover, design, and layout by Donald Ward

Printed and bound in Canada

Canadian Cataloguing in Publication Data

Safarik, Allan, 1948-

How I know the sky is a river

0-9682256-4-0

PS8587.A245H68 1999 C811'.54 C99-920229.49
PR9199.3.S153H68 1999

The Hagios Press
314 – 1121 College Drive
Saskatoon SK S7N 0W3

Contents

Introduction

Most of my life I have been interested in writing poems. It really started as a teenage preoccupation when I discovered, in myself, a contemplative side that could be tuned in to provide relief from dealing with the chaos of the real world and the repetitious cycles that dominate our daily habits. The dwelling of self contained a private room that soon became a sanctuary for the meditative pursuit of writing poetry.

My teachers thought I was taking notes when really I was perfectly disguised working on something else. That *something else* grew steadily through the years, until an avocation turned into an obsession and finally became a half-assed occupation. Along the way I have been lucky enough to find continuous employment in the allied trades; the broader field of writing, editing, and publishing that fuel the book industry.

The poems in this volume are selected shorter poems from five previous volumes that were published by a handful of small presses in British Columbia and Ontario. They include Blackfish Press, Porcupine's Quill, Oolichan Books, Polestar Press, and Black Moss. I owe the publishers of these companies — Brian Brett, Tim Inkster, Ron Smith, Julian Ross, Michelle Benjamin and Marty Gervais — a great deal. In addition, I have included fifteen new poems written in Dundurn, Saskatchewan in the winters of '97 and '98.

It is common for poets to be visited by a presence, a voice, a visitor, a spiritual advisor, an Angel, or to experience other manifestations, such as automatic writing. Poems are essentially gifts inspired by a mysterious process between the writer and what is appropriately called the *muse.*

I saw an Angel standing behind the choir in a church in North Burnaby, British Columbia, when I was nine years old. The voices of dead people I have known talk to me at times. Often I answer back, but I am more interested in the living than the dead. My church is the bus station, the truck stop on a long stretch of highway, a back road in the middle of July, or a small-town hockey rink on a Friday night in February. I wander on odd Saturday afternoons in the bookstores on Queens Street in Toronto or Pender Street in Vancouver. I'm there in a corner of the photograph of the Blue House on the hill above the beach in White Rock, BC, in a field of oats in the middle of summer near Dundurn, at an auction in a barn at Lonesome (bidding on Grandpa Clampett's last painting), stopping at Little Pine, passing through Big River, broken down at 42 below zero near Findlater or reading a magazine in the library at Humboldt.

Life is a river. Time takes the place of water. Images and fragments of people and places flow by. Poetry is a kind of spiritual language, usually with an *ism* attached to it. The doctrine of construction. I think the only *ism* worth its salt is *humanism*. Writing poetry is an essential habit that has taken over my life. These shorter poems are the poems of free moments that have expired on buses, in motels, airports, cafes, and endless nights of bingeing. These are the pulses of DNA leaping out from the end of my doodling pen into notebooks and eventually finding their way into various editions of my work. In this poet's mind the poems written over so many years have blurred in a pattern not unlike a quilt; words, ideas, and images rehearsed and arranged like colours and textures in the fabric of the landscape or the social world. Pieces have been left here and there in my small pantheon of poetry books. Sometimes I think the river of life is a stream of dreams and visions in time, traveling through space. Like memories and nostalgia, liquid in human brain cells, flooding the mind with torrents of clarity. Poems are like children, sooner or later they come home and take a walk around the old neighbourhood. Alas, time can also be a powerful eraser, softening the shadow of the emotional life or rubbing it off the page.

Poems are neither artifacts or photographs, but in a way they are similar. Each artifact, photo, or poem is an individual entity. When they are joined with their ilk they are altered by the process and become part of something else. The artifact is a cultural indicator, the photo a virtual witness, and the poem a voice in the text. In the case of poetry, the individual poem is often a fragment in an evolving process that is not linear or best defined in a strict chronological framework. My definition of a shorter poem varies; from a few words in duration to a poem of one page in length. With that in mind these poems have been revisited and edited into another arrangement. One that rekindles and redefines relationships and associations while shuffling the cards in the deck before dealing another hand. The arbitrary is always sneaking in at the deadline.

Some of the poems in this volume are exceedingly short. Sometimes in literary jargon they are referred to as *tiny poems*. I prefer to think of them as *micro poems* because they invoke visual impressions in an emotional way while delving into the *micro-universal*. I think of the *micro poem* as the starter motor that turns over a larger engine. They are the impulses that ignite the process of poetry. Micro poems residing quietly on book pages are often conveniently dropped between larger poems to satisfy the vagaries of editing and design.

The selecting of shorter poems in this edition is intended to give them new life in a different context in a volume that only the loving hands of small press publishing can provide. Thanks to John Livingstone Clark and Donald Ward, who remain fully rooted in the finer traditions of small press publishing, The Saskatchewan Arts Board for its meaningful support, *Western People* for publishing several of the new poems in this selection, *Event* and *Spitball*.

This book is dedicated to William Hoffer (1943 - 1997); bookseller, publisher, list maker, agent, art patron, essayist, bridge and billiard player. Devoted friend and enemy of writing and publishing in Canada. Never dull, more often provocative or profound. A man with an uncompromising vision. He worked hard at trying to motivate us to get better, sometimes we didn't let him down.

In memory of

William Hoffer

Almost an Epigram

I was taken into the light
by an immaculate bird
It shook its feathered
coat of flames
in the morning sky

Everywhere the sun
evaporated in the grass
Careless as a lover
I saw the bird of summer
waking in your hair

May Day

this month passes its time
on earth, a love poem
of tiny unfurling grape leaves

summer flowers untouched by rain
grinning pyromaniacs
are the pride of the earth

Another May Day Poem

Flowers and armaments
make good bedfellows

On the wide boulevards, tanks
drive over cherry blossoms

"The cemeteries look great
this time of year"

Above the Bones

When we talked again
I spoke the wrong language
The dead unmemorable air
that fell from my parched lips
choked-up from blood
of an already condemned voice
The words, bitten seeds
dribbling on my shirt front
stain me blue and bitter

And you, dear unassailable
woman with beautiful shoulders
and unblemished logic
walk away, glasses tilted
on the sun rippling water-
fall of uncut hair
The pear-coloured taste
of your flesh up for grabs

Moon in a Fraction of the Sky

Wanted to make small
harmless wounds on you
in the sentimental night

Wanted to invade your dreams
with the army of myself
marching down your limbs

Wanted to see the animal
of you waking in the dawn
from the nest of your sleeping

Wanted these things and more
the many ways love conquers
all the sins of my keeping

In the Fumbling of My Desire

Making useless moves
I want to start over telling
you though I have already
said too much. Begin again
by clearing my throat
It goes badly from the first
sentence until the last
You finish all my thoughts

The liquor calms my peril
the erasing ice-cubes
the weight of it in the glass
warming and cold like our memories
In the fumbling of my desire
I pour you, even your laughter
back into the bottle
without spilling a drop

The Definition of Our Love

Wounded, small and gray
with a leaking hole
in its pigeon breast
It flies around the room
bumping furniture
thumping into windows

like a padded fist

The Rehearsal of Objects

Growing from the earth
toward the sun,
a tree is an image
of certain happiness.

To perceive this image
we must be immobile
like the tree.

When we are moving
it is the tree
which becomes
the spectator.

It is witness, equally
in the shape of chairs,
tables and doors,
to the more or less
agitated spectacle
of our life.

The tree,
having become
a coffin disappears
into the earth.

And when
it is transformed
into fire
it vanishes
into the air.

—found in the prose of Rene Magritte

The Bird Nailed To His Wings

there is strength in gentleness
take the bird soaring above his life
green trees below waking in the sun
wind disturbing quiet water
air rushing through his sieve of feathers
like your mouth where everything
returns to take on pleasure
the beautiful wings of your hands
nailed to the gauntlet of your wrists
I hunger for you around the blueness
of the wide open earth

there is strength in gentleness
I would soar for you
if these flapping hands of mine could fly
many nights I went down trying
lost in the mountains of my desire
in the morning when everything whole
was chained in the impossible light
your wings spread into the heat
of the luminous summer's day
and you disappeared in the unreturning sky
leaving me here nailed to my clumsy feet

Long Shadows

There is exactitude
in an unmade bed

the abstract
impression you left
merges into my
absence

wind tears
the curtains
from the open
window

the moon is a
faint hangnail
in the watery
blue sky

Turning Out the Double

— and life, when was it truly your own?
When are truly what we are?
In truth we are not, we are never

I took the morning sun
from the innocent sky
hid it in my pocket
so you couldn't wake up
even tomorrow if you wanted
to remember your dreams

I picked the stars
from their black vine
extinguished them
in a bucket of water
so you couldn't fall asleep
and forget who you are

The Transparent Iris

Genitalia of the flower
There is no blue
Pale as you
On the edge
Of many broad swords
Blood of the air
In your watery stems
Bees insult you
With their ragged feet
Innocent rain splits
You with cold
Indifference
But the sun
Comes again
Opens you
Joyously
Like a secret lover
Your blueness
Trembling slightly
In the wind

The Brooch

Tiny blue crabs
in Kensington Market
grapple thin air

with sculptured claws
like flames spending
a temporary life

I buy one lethargic
specimen, clasp it
flickering to your dress

The Meadow of Blessed Cows

I tell you cows are beautiful creatures
with their chewing chewing chewing countenances
and the compact yet bulky nature of their thinking
Ideas move through them slowly like a hesitating
ball of solid matter propelled by stomach gas
It's almost a holy ritual, the blessed way
green grass miraculously turns into meat

I thought of none of these complicated things
when making drunken love with you in the meadow
we were interrupted by an audience of curious
tail swishing bovines flipping dumb-cane ears
The gods of red meat blankly staring down
bless us with their drooling blunt noses
and their stupid thick tongues

The Bloodletting

Lend me your heart she said
pulling it from my chest
Naturally the apparatus
of my breathing went along as well
Releasing the swaying palms of my blood

It poured from me into her hands
down around her feet
Her dress was soaked with it
Soon her face and her hair
were streaked and matted

The people she met in the street
asked if they could help
as she walked by clutching
my heart to her breast
like a struggling infant

After a time when it calmed
she wrapped it in a shaggy blanket
sang it nursery rhymes
fed it warm bottles of milk
Took it to her bed

Lend me your heart she said
pulling it from my chest
And though my body and I were left
behind, my heart beating in the rooms
of her love, became her child

Angel Fish

Is there anything more beautiful
in the sky than water
Blue eye of the earth
staring into the memory of space
like an enormous bait

The world is my tomb
Coral-tinted ivory forest
Inventory of exotic shells
lingering in the shallows
If they are the flowers

I am the butterfly of the sea

Winter Sun

A few miserable sparrows
hop among the barren grape vines
I put the cage of my hand around
the winter sun. The birds leave it empty
The cat hiding in the restless leaves
gnaws happily on a mole's pink head
Fat little mole body chugging away
like a breast-stroking engine

Death is perfunctory to the domesticate
The well fed cat extracts the gruesome
toll of cruelty and mutilation
with an innocent flicking tail

Nature is perfect in desire!
I catch nothing but the cold light
in the cage of my hand
Bring it in, warm it by the fire

The Owl

People think the owl wise
because he looks remarkably similar
to the house cat, who is no dummy
and because he is endowed
with all the tools of the judge

In truth the Chinese call owl
the cat bird and though he eats
the same little mammals as cat
and has sharp feline ears
he is not very bright

But don't pity the owl
when the song birds find him
roosting in the daytime
the invective and hatred he endures
would make a wiser creature paranoid

Not the owl, his reversal is
swooping in pillow dark madness
No time for pleas or emotion
he sentences each rodent impartially
with his legal beak, judicial talons

How I Know the Sky Is A River

the mountain ash
is covered
with spawn

Crab

The crab scurries
sideways revving
his eye beads
Antennae twinkling
Ultra robot claws

if crabs could live
for long in air
they'd soon be feeding
in the streets

crabs and dogs
fighting it out
all over the city

freeway crabs
fat with plunder
move relentlessly
across the continent

imagine the day
the first crab
scuttles into
Saskatoon

Saskatoon

this European river
passing like vodka
under black iron bridges
sweet green city
on the Danube, the Volga

the magpies here
are wiser than dust
with their witty glass eyes
and ballroom suits —
drunk all the time!

Maybe old people die
and turn into magpies
the one in the elm tree
telling me a tragic story
about her useless daughter

Octopus

The octopus
escapes
the fish plant
by forcing
its own matter
for several days
through a drain
pipe

Comes up
onto the land
throwing spears
wrapping the cups
on his arms
around the sun lit
friction of air

Birds flash
down at him
a blizzard
of yellow feet
slashing bills
wrung necks

Smarter than
a city dog
brain-testicle
hiding in the
scrotum purple
discoloured skin

Plastic eyes
quivering
in the tortured
ease of living
minus bones

Mad Dogs Are Beautiful

Walking by
I put
a bullet
in the
Doberman's
stiletto
head
through
his eye
blew his
crown in
like a can
of beans

Walking by
I said
all this
quietly
under
my breath
dropping
a wiener
with a
detonator
among
his toy
bones

Walking by
hung
with
triple
hooks
dripping
cyanide
I slowly
offer
him
my
glove-
less
hand

Red Parrots In the Blue Jungle

Of wounding teeth
there are plenty of stories

The dental deformities
which caused certain Bengal tigers
to become man-eating Gods
stripping and devouring
blood soaked clothes

Septic holes pouring forth
from the mauled victims
(who were almost always
carried off alive)
filling up with cries
of tropical birds,
coughing deer

Of your wounding teeth
grazing like small hatchets
on the pastures of my throat
And my larger jungle ones
following your outline
down the hills
of darkness

The Human Factor

Some men
are so desperate
for company
they would sleep with dogs
or sheep or occasionally
with a porcupine

porcupines, however
having no equivalent
(apart from other
porcupines)
lead extremely
lonely lives

dogs, universal
theologians of sexual
perversion and technique
if they have any brains
give porcupines
ice in winter

even the amorous sheep
with their reputation
for soulful eyes,
juicy rumps
bound away

The Afterthought

Chinatown
fish peddler
chops
rock cod
and red cod
with cleaver
on smooth
wooden block

just missing
fingers
Divinity rises
and falls

Icarus

I

the moulting robin
fat
ragged
on the fence post

II

flying-up
a ripe berry
hanging in the sky

III

a flame
in the green tree

Between a Man and a Woman Was a Sail of Skin

—for BTB

Ocean and sky have empathy
as bird and bird
have common wing

A fire after dark
is a hole is a star
is an illusion
as clear as wind

the stone is
as the fossil
inside was alive
a shape imprinted

an uncommon fragment
in a well
deeper than its water

Yellow and the Grave Sea

Two shore birds becalmed
under heavy grey weather
pregnant summer sky
great yellow stain
sulks and stalks
the wide hard sand slopes
all night beside
  the silent sea
  we have heard the sound
under a moon full and hidden
the earth's sail hangs
over our heads
and the moon's open wound
sings to the ocean

Monsters, grey whales —
barnacle encrusted
elephant hide
opens a trembling pathway
the sea sound flowing
like blood from the loud wound

The great bulk of whale
is the moon's tear
(lick of salt)
is the moon turning
and rolling
under a mile of ocean
turning and burning

in the fiery throat
that is cold and deep
and blue and deeper a blue
than sky
is the ocean that sings in the heart
of the fire
is the fire that sings in the heart
of the whale

The One-Eyed Song of Love

One is all I need
One eye to let in the light
To let my face laugh or cry
One eye to open the skin of sleep
One man, one eye, one life
One day at a time
Two are for the protection of one

And if the other be gone
Let it look on the stabbed point
Of a thorn flying like a bird
From the grass

Living in my face in my brain
Jewel of water and blood
Brilliant egg of flesh
Camera of cameras
How lucky I was to have you
for even one hour

Two Eyes of the Faithless Dog

Faith dwells in the dog
In and around his panting head
Prints of sweat on ancient leather
or faded curtains
on basement window walls

The dog who killed chickens
Chomping into their backs (the snap of an old
man's mouth on a three pound cigar)
Went to jail for ripping a child's arm
And maybe was gassed.
A certain lie —

For his death was uncommonly simple
as yellow liquid in a white cup
His little faith in people
left back temporal memories
Faded raspberry teeth marks
Nothing more

Deer

the deer
are without faces

but have
shapes and graces

men kill deer
to own
and touch
the skin
for an instant

two deer hanging
in the garage
on silver meat hooks
my father
in a grey wool shirt
sweating and heaving
his shoulder
into the meat saw

I as a child
ran screaming
from the whine
of steel teeth
through bone

and I dreamt
so many nights
that I too hung
on silver meat hooks

Knock Knock the Air Is Empty of Sound

The woman
in the coma
was in the seventh
year of her enclosure
dreaming a novel:

pure landscape
and ether.
There were no
human beings

She was in
the second year
of describing
a solitary
tree

and now
it was burning
on a hill
into the layers
of darkness

lighting
the night sky

It was so
beautiful
she had been
crying
for joy

Tale of the Firefly

— for Heidi

They fly in the fantasy of sparks
spread out blinking in the open sky

Fleas on the hot green body of the lapped dog
Tree Gods dropping fleshy cigar ashes

Neon Cosmic Nomads carry the suitcase of light
from the heavens white and naked to the heavy earth

In the skin caves of my hands, just an insect
the cool seed of a melon plucked from its meat

So slowly they move the pulsing abdomens in air
On off, stop go, here now, there then, I you

The six year old child standing in the garden
filled his wide mouthed jar with star ships

Luminous heart-beats in a glass walled prison
Hoping to light a way by lantern's jaw —

He could not keep them long;
The sadness shone through him

After the Rainbow

Two children in a yellow kitchen
as kitchens warm mellow places
should be yellow for children

with a box of broken crayons
red and orange worn to the nub

nothing profound: a lop sided
sail boat on a too blue sea
and a rainbow that is such a lie
it hurts the eyes

but there is wind ever slight
moving through the gaudy light
the ringing of a tiny bell

innocent bright as hell
this picture never seen before
never seen again splashes laughter
changes what is real, changes

what is not, in the garden
of their minds growing

Do Birds Live in a Blue World

— (a child asks) for Jeremy & Jevon

No, Theirs is red and green
Eyes that prick from high
In a cold cross current
of wind that drifts like water
And has a silver side

Eyes that see inside the world
from outside its skin
With a fine penetrating glance
define moving things as quick
as a dog smells his dinner

Birds have feathers carefully muted
as snow. That grow on their bodies
like leaves. Each feather is a charm
different from the next

But birds bruise easily
and die quickly from shock.
They are made to fly

And when they can't they hide
still in a secret spot
Calling to the air. Soon
they are quiet and lost

Birds have a green and red world
because when the frost saws
into the grass

Their tiny hearts encased
in a miracle hollow of bones
Tick like fine jeweled watches

And they fly far away

Tokens from the Heart

The robins
in winter
look foolish
in the snow

The cat knows
(claws out like ice)
all about song
birds

I put him out
purring
into the dark
night

Rock River Poem

Lightning bugs
ignite in the
tender night

Big yellow carp
swarm after
mallard ducklings

Meat in the Silo

The soon to be butchered pig
feels nothing
but the jerking wire on his trotter
and the sadness
that wallops him in the air

Strange anesthesia —
Truth baptized by terror.
He understands clearly
his death is payment
for all that lovely eating

If you doubt this
watch his eyes
when he discovers the knife
in the hand at his throat

Horticulture

Horrified, I see
a horde of aphids
on my roses
And I watch
for hours
the relationship
between the sucking
masses
and their master
ants
marching
about
a herd
of fat green swine

How basic
the logic
of politics
is to all creatures:
the order
the production
of supplies, goods
and services —
the movement
and consumption
Only man
takes a profit

Overhead
the sun
in the sky
shines
like a stolen
watch

The Duality of One

What humours the worm?
Miscast in his rubbery slumber
he languishes on the cement
slowly cooking
under the summery sun
There in the odd clotted
segments of the day
a part of him lopped off
wandered another way

I too grow again
When my bones are breaking
under the hot stone
My life divides; the part
that stayed here to talk with you
and the bloody piece
I kept for myself —
They are different but the same
like the halves of the worm
crawling away from the one

Pastoral

What the mirror imagines
it gives back in the clear unreality
of the moment

In this silken dawn
a gentle rain falls down from the grey flesh
languishing in the sky

What the land has taken
does not deign to take the shape
of the land

Everything seems flat and emptying
Bare trees stick up from the mud
in the fashion of tent poles

And the horse's cock
extends below his belly
like a handshake
draining the fields

God Loves Us Like Earthworms Love Wood

Try hard to make my words
more concerned with humans
less of the natural world
and my self-projection
coming through from the Sun
The moving figure casts a shadow
We are all starved creatures
gasping in the garden of vapours

Opened like a wine skin
We last less than half-an-hour
The room is sharp
painfully in focus
Everything bold and square
The mail lies on the kitchen table
Water runs over the sink
The toilet is full with blood

Stroked by a corridor of light
that black cat sleeps on the bed

And the beautiful head is singing
My sorrow is a dried-up river
My love is a burnt pile of papers
My faith hovers in the light
by my closing eyes
My pity is for the living flowers
clotted in the humid air
pieces of bright red sponge

The beautiful head is singing
God loves us like earthworms love wood
long after the body is dead

Pitt River Road

On the wire
clumps of ice
mistaken for birds

the man with frozen hands
repairing his car
early morning
side-of-the-road
surrounded
by desolate fields
of paper corn
and a hedge-row
of hazel trees

Look again
and you'll see
those birds
were real enough
disguised as ice

The Thought

wanted to look at your face
in the middle of the blackest night
wind blowing in the bedroom walls
thin window glass taking the push of it
slipping against the room like a sail

waking up in a cold sweat
covered by a snowfall of blankets
Sunday morning in another time zone
I flick on my Bic lighter forgetting
nothing is left but the presence

wanted it to leave for seven months
it stayed nearby speaking quietly
thought you were there, you were gone
down the roadway, left me holding down
the bed sheets, waiting for the blindfold

Tree in Moonlight

there is
a scaffold
of twigs

over the
blankness
of the earth

take this
tree holding
my neck

here I
can see
bloody clouds

making war
in the bowl
of the sky

The Debt

All good things paid in full
bad nights thrown in gratis
My intelligence reeks of intemperate ideas
among shattered verbs, indefinite punctuation
a little parable

From the sun's incredible heat
Icarus came home burning
darkness speared him

Light blinds, water drowns
The mind attempts suffocation in broad daylight
wills itself behaviour for the good of the body
telling it the mood doesn't change the weather
or cancel buds on the trees

Yellow Bird

Urgent yellow bird
species unidentified
beating fancy scarves
around the breeze

something damaged
makes the flapping
a pitiful banner
cries reach the street

Striped cat rushes in
and away with lemon feathers
bouquet of strange flowers
boasting in its jaws

fluttering tail
pinions broken
neck an awkward question mark
bird returned like lost property

Does this quickly
disappearing drama
have the confidence
of the landscape?

beak opening, closing
with a metallic snap
black eye
pointed at the sky

Mystery

They found a hand
in the ravine this morning
clutching a revolver
A right hand removed neatly
just above the wrist
maybe by a fine-toothed saw
It was wearing a gold ring
set with a black stone
on the index finger
The lifeline seemed to run
forever across the palm
white and puffy
from the dampness in the grass

Who knows how these things pass?
A severed hand turns up
in the city park
holding a loaded pistol
The police go door to door
seeking information
no matter how trivial
Several people finger neighbours
for a number of reasons including
violent tempers and shifty eyes
One man even tries to take credit
Somehow in the confusion
while evidence is being gathered
the ring disappears

The Price of Loneliness

All the amusing
stories
I keep to myself
jokes
in the telling
grow weary
in the silence
of the curtains
and the texture
of the paint

there was a spider
here one night
cruising
the baseboards
I posed
the central
question
of my dilemma

he answered
with his
eloquent
black
legs

Meaning of Time

This morning the sun broke
the porch window pushing
its way into the kitchen
Flowering cherry trees spill
pink joy into windy streets
The confident tap, tapping
of the blind man finding
his way down narrow stairs
becomes inquisitive scratching

He might be asking pavement
for direction or pausing
to inhale the perfumed air
drawing conclusions from the cane's
wiry voice sweeping the bricks
testing every corner of possibility
feeling the sense of the hour
The second hand doesn't stop
traveling for darkness or light

Swordfish Steaks

At the grill
coals glow
for the sake
of the fish

I thought
we were
a recipe
that would
satisfy
the feast

It's all
unnecessary
bothering
with white
heat
crumbling
ash

They'll cook
faster
more evenly
if you
simply
lay them
on my
forehead

The Ruler

In her cups
she said
what you've got
between your legs
is more interesting
than what's between
your stupid ears
and even that
doesn't really
measure up

I thought
in my most
sensitive mood
she was
after my mind
now I find out
too late
I'm just
another plus
minus figure
in a pair
of trousers

Mimicry of Birds at War

I found these words, assembled them in space
The machine moves along the line
with authority, making
important black marks
A blank field fills with ideas
All of them untried and unregistered
A sudden movement, everything spills
back into the pool of chance
Pages fall still on the floor

The secondary message could not
be verbally translated
Birds on the wires speaking
through the voice of nests
repeated transpacific telephone calls
There was a great deal of repetition
and mass regurgitations
In the morning, white fields
illustrated calligraphy of crows

Bulova

In the end, time ruins everything
Reality is always moving on
to the next destination.
Those who wish to stay young
are sentenced by gravity.
When things are going better than ever,
a fluke happens;
against million to one odds
an innocent gardener
is destroyed by a coffee cup
tossed from a plane flying
at ten thousand feet

Why are real tragedies humorous?
Because they are arbitrary
things happening to unknown
people with unusual names
I read about them in newspapers
The worker who lost it
when he swallowed a bee while painting
the flagpole on the Hancock Tower.
The woman in Portland who cut off
her husband's head with a chainsaw
when he got stuck in the wall
and abusively ordered her
to cut in the wrong direction

A robot in a Japanese car plant
stabbed its master to death
with a strip of chrome.
Time passes all things through dust.
We wait, hoping the bomb
will not go off, detonated
by some foolproof system
invented by time

The Sand Line

There is no way
to leave the ocean
the armoured brown crab
knows it, dropping
its shell on the line

Purple starfish prove
the universe is a black ocean
filled with light
dogfish send green eyes
locating hunger

Small slender fish
turn slivers of ice
rising and falling surf
diving sea birds
bring up bottom

Corks popping
from blue-fringed waves
evening clouds
red sun
along the sand line

The Voyage Home

There is no advantage
with the sea, impatient
victors are always
taking off in haste
without glancing at the glass
or tuning in the planets

The drunks who hit rocks
always seem to find trouble
in clear unforgiving weather
Maybe they forgot to steer
or made up their minds
by trusting the wrong light

Or got talking too long
about the end of the voyage
cursing bad food or someone
falls asleep at the wheel
and bingo, bottom is touching
foreheads with blue fingers

Sunflower

the sun
on a stem
in solitary
idleness

The Shrine

Bean fields are holy places
where sun worships green
a snake in the bean fields —
good luck unless
a yellow cobra
then very bad luck
if its temper is disturbed

At night pickers
in shacks hear
the patter of rat feet
on the rooftops and the thirsty
gliding sound the snake makes
chasing it down, the bean
fields smell like heaven

Nobody, but the rat fears dying
when the bean fields flower
in the holiest place of the sun

Wood Bugs

Little grey hunchbacks
with a nervous
abundance of legs
medieval battle helmets
dropping out
from rotten wood

When they jacked
the house up
from its lamentable
foundations
legions of wood
bugs marched
on White Rock

Sure they're welcome
to their dank dark
wooden homes
making wood into dirt
is as honourable
a profession as turning
lead into gold
or pigs into sausages

The Cage

the opening in the cage
is not larger than a fist
a hand pushed through
could see light

do you ever feel threatened
by everything in the past?
why the cage left the bird open?
why or where the bird flew?

Perfect Zero

the sun has begun
its fade-out
blue hills mark
edges of the sky
the moon stayed
all day

Fleas

In the summer of the holiest feast
old clothes, straw beds were burned
fleas became an element of dust
In the dark fields of eternity
a city was besieged by armies of stars

Fleas from the body of Christ
lived through centuries
hiding in hair, feeding on human blood
Cloth smoldered, straw beds withered
When he died there on the cross
fleas gave up the ship
dropping onto Roman soldiers
who paused on the road to stare
The stars went on glittering
with cricket sounds
Citizens of Rome were infested
by ravaging hordes of biting fleas
Even those wearing the finest
Chinese silk were not immune

All the Roman deities nearly scratched
themselves to death, slaves rejoiced
seeing gods turning into mortals
standing with senators and whores
beside the heaping pyres of rosewood

Approximate Nightmare

The sky blows up.
Lava is pouring from the clouds
Fiery pterodactyls descend from the jet stream.
Citizens of White Rock make their way to the pier
I go back for the cat, check to see the back door
  is locked.
By the time I reach the waterfront the pier
is burning like a pile of toothpicks in an ashtray.
People are crowded together on the decks of a
  passenger ship
pulling away from the breakwater
I see you on the stern in yachting clothes,
popping a bottle of champagne.
The band strikes an up-tempo
samba version of *Amazing Grace*.
Everybody waves goodbye.

U. S. Customs

Lost and found briefly
at the border,
the guards made us
sit in silence
brooding about our guilt
they brewed coffee

nothing would give me
more pleasure than to strip
search you both
and find whatever it is
you're hiding

I adjusted the drugged
parrot in my trousers
pushing it further
down the pant leg
if the snake wakes up
we're lost for good

no outstanding warrants
or drug convictions
he returned our I. D.
your underwear stayed on
clinging in the v
of your baby panda

We fooled him with phony
looks and selfish manners
I wanted to scream
Hey buddy, we're the real
thing, big-time poachers
wearing wild animals
under our clothes

White Birds

Left the coast at daybreak
Watched white birds veering out
over the bay disappear in the fog
covering the view of islands
Obscuring corrugated water

I was drowning looking at water
Couldn't find appropriate words
to master changes in the weather
Silence is a stone weapon
No sound exists to stop it for long

Passing one last time in fall
through shadowy mountains
New snow on the glacier
bright pile of feathers
between granite peaks
Blue walls rise into the sun

Nothing restless about mountains
Light leaves quickly pausing
at the edges of jagged rock
Finding a dislocated soul
in a small pocket of time
Darkness comes slamming down

Motel Window

He wants to steal a car
take a long ride in the country
and make out in the moonlight

She wants to go back to the party
catch the band's last set
and go home with her sister

I want to get back to sleep
but their voices are playing
tennis in my double bed

Listen I yell, why not steal
the car after the band stops
and take out the sister

Picket Fence

Old dog
panting
in a glimpse
of shade

Far Field

The plough breaks up the earth
white birds dipping behind
clouds of wings, frenzied cries

I watch the green tractor for hours
moving in the distance to the edge
nearly vanishing on the horizon

It returns dragging a ribbon of dust
The kid says, "Look it's pulling the sky"
In the transformation the birds are lost

Double Rainbow

Long shafts of slanted light
shine on yellow fields
Big raindrops hit the dust

Self-Portrait in a Field of Oats

Nothing calmer than shoulder
high oats on a summer day
This field touches the horizon
Brushing the sky in every direction
Grain gathering heat shakes slightly
under the weight of the sun

Crickets crawling on cracked earth
exchange bursts of eccentric music
Wind rips across miles of grass
The issue complicated by colour
I walk back to the car on the road
Change the film to black and white

Impossible memories torch the mind
like a match head igniting on a coin
in the folds of a jacket pocket
My psyche walks into the picture
Waits twenty seconds for the camera
to record my transient image

Could not escape painful years
How they fill in sadness and shame
with new people and different places
along the hours of many roads
The picture, a fragment in passing
left on a frame of film in a sea of oats

Choke Cherries

Black fruit, shriveled leaves
White from gravel dust
Blue and red cloth offerings
Solitude of a holy place
Branches for arrow shafts

Wandered looking at coloured stones
among cactus squatting in the sand
Picked up a deer skull pierced
by sharp grass, sun ticking like
a forgotten element on a stove

Simple things easily located in time
A long thin distorted shadow
Spirits in the choke cherry woods
Black juice staining the sky
Welts from bending branches

Swainson's Hawk

A dot on the blue sky
passing across white clouds
drifts down over the fields
crafting wings around air currents
methodically sweeping the ground
until it sees the gopher's silhouette
caught in a nervous movement
standing upright at its hole

The attitude of wings
in a brief fragment of time
drops talons into the equation
the bird on course at speed
aiming at its paralyzed target
hits it with opened razors
A small explosion of dust
and blood on twisting feathers

Prairie Jackfish Recipe

Northern Pike, Jackfish
Alias: Slough Shark or
Prairie Alligator

Catch one ten pounder
on a red and white spoon
Cut into fillets
Marinate overnight

In a large crock
Mix a 750 ml bottle of red wine
with a bottle of vodka
Two cups dry Spanish sherry
Add a 26 oz bottle
of Wiser's Deluxe

In the morning carefully
extract the fillets
Feed them to the cat
Drink the marinade

Jig Time

Spent an hour removing a barbed hook
from my new shirt after retrieving it
from a thick clump of willow
Prying it out from under two slabs of rip rap
Tossed a weighted jig head with feathers
Nearly hooked a misguided seagull
on a small prairie reservoir
The line broke when I caught bottom
and lost Mister Twister
Mosquitoes attack at dusk
from behind a Bloody Mary sunset
Hovering in feeding frenzy

If I slashed the air with a knife
only stars would show through
So many lures to catch the eye
in the blinking constellations
I try a few last futile casts
with a wobbly diving spoon
armed with a treble hook
Falling stars flash and dance
Crazy bait in the absolute
Crashing smooth water

Summer of Rain

By mid-August
cucumbers refused to form
Peppers still sprinkled
with tiny white flowers
started dropping leaves
Tomatoes made sad skeletons
among the garden sticks
Tall tasseled corn stalks
grew a blizzard of leaves
without a single cob

Garfield died standing up
washing his hands
at the bathroom sink
I thought of his soul
rising in the dust
against the thunder heads
while his sad face stared
blankly out the window glass

Big trees of light
in the distant sky
The rumbling of summer
passing overhead
In a lost season
good enough to die

Mule Deer on the Hanley Road

Constant wind travels in a hurry
across the vast cultivated prairie
Trees in the hedge rows bend
and sway in permanent homage
Small dust storms boil on fallow ground
White gulls soaring in blue air
pass through high sparse clouds
Tumble weeds catch barb wire fences
The car fighting head winds
on loose gravel handles like a boat
on a stretch of bad water

Deer on the Hanley Road hesitate
looking away at some distant object
Big ears flipping in the breeze
They bound across on springy legs
Leaping a six foot wire fence
as if a semi-invisible barrier
casually left in place
There must be a million miles of wire
strung across the empty country
Thin edge of the horizon stapled
along the edge of the wind

The Attic

After midnight in the old house
Fat black cat thumping on the staircase
Grandpa's snoring buzzes through the ceiling
Constant creaking in the walls
interrupted by clock chimes

Sudden alarm from the firehall
Two trucks roar down Penticton Street
A car door slams in the dark
Chinese voices converse in the alley
Neighbours, home from the restaurant
They'll be gone back to work
again before I wake

Grandma gets up in her room
I turn out the bedside light until the toilet flushes
She puts out the cat, scolding her in Czech,
about bringing home birds,
before going back to bed

Pale moonlight in an attic window
Seated at the treadle sewing machine
looking through a pile of tintype photos,
legal documents in foreign languages
Many ribbons and wax seals
A box of ancient fountain pens
Bone and tortoise shell

Soft cooing from pigeons
roosting on rooftops
spread the murmur of sleep
I fall into feathers,
Soothing sounds of boxcars
shunting on the waterfront
Foghorns in the harbour

Grandpa's Lunch

A slab of head cheese
one pound of brains
blue cheese on rye bread
pickled herring
salted poppy seed buns
a dozen Old Style on ice
one large Cuban cigar

The Ice Man

We ran after the ice man's truck
when it passed the reservoir
dribbling our soccer ball
between the white lines
down the centre of the street
bouncing it off board fences
We caught up to him on Boundary Road
and begged for the long slivers of ice
he carved with his chisel
Struck by a wooden mallet

He picked-up a big block with tongs
swung it over his back
and climbed the back stairs
to the kitchen at the Anglican church
We sat in the shade of the truck
When he came back the sweat on his brow
soaked through the brown slouch cap
the sun played with the edges
of his black rubber apron
while the ice slipped through
our hands like the days of summer

Myth's Taken

The man with the knife
in his hand is my father
See how carefully he slits
the bellies of salmon
Each fish a tube
silver and Pacific blue

Blood crawls over the floor
slowly building a pool
He strips the layers of orange eggs
and thick clouded milts
white as the death of flesh
Splot, dropping them into cans
for Fukuyama Egg Man

With one twist of his left hand
rips out the red gills
Huge pieces of fruit
Breathing machines
tossed underhand
slow motion end-over-end
collars of blood bounce
into the gut barrel

See how carefully he paces the knife
Tending it like a gunman
or the trainer wrapping
the boxer's fists
Beautiful fish on ice
cold deadly perfect charms

Black Swans

Some things never break down
from the rays of the sun
A black car stares
out from a driveway
It's worn down like an old smile
The sun has been working
on it for half a century
Absorbing the shimmering
metallic finish
crushing the fenders
with the weight of light

The Nuns from Seton Academy
playing baseball on the field
beside the reservoir
could hit and field
they ran at the crack of the bat
Slid head first into second base
We called them the black swans
as they whipped the ball
around the infield

The sun beat them senseless
in their long robes
They withered soon enough
Dust crept over the diamond
fading the black from their lives
They gathered in the shade of the trees
for a cool drink of water
dabbing it on their foreheads

Graceful as swans
We never saw their necks uncovered

Unreasonable Doubt

Every Saturday morning for thirty years
a little brown car pulled up
in front of the house
My mother bought magazines
from Jehovah Witnesses
Awake and *Watchtower*
fit perfectly into the
bottom of the bird cage

She handed them twenty cents
for two stapled magazines
The dog starting barking
when they brought up
spiritual matters
Snapping at persistence
Mother closed the door firmly
on unnecessary conversations

She didn't want to disappoint
anybody working for God
The bird was happy enough
with a clean new bed spread
When he heard their knock
Beating his head incessantly
against the shiny bell

The Patient

He had slight grey hands
that covered his mouth
when he coughed

They were the size
of small pigeons
roosting in the sheets
When he talked
they flew around the room
I wanted them to find
a place to land
They wouldn't stop
struggling against
the window's glass

The nurse came in
telling him it was time
for his prep

He walked me to the elevator
in his bathrobe, left me
laughing with a story
about the old neighbourhood
I knew by his eyes,
the colour of sand,
he was preparing to depart

"Don't worry if things
don't work out
I'll send you a message
from the other side"
When I shook his hand
I felt the bird in it
pecking at my palm

Wondering about the pigeons
dangling on his wrists
If I would see them in the sky

Bird of Prey

The banker is going
over my cold accounts
like a hungry vulture perched
on a coagulating gopher
"I'm afraid the bank can't. . . "
Before he finished
I was up shaking his hand
with dead white fingers

Bits of clotted blood,
matted hair, cotton batting
blew out from the hole
in the back of my head
His hunched form defecated
on the glass topped table

Shooting Gallery

Shooting our Daisy bb gun
at Graham crackers or the
flames on birthday candles
held by clothes pegs
against the basement wall
Looking through the peep sight
at shadowy flickering targets
my brother and me arguing
under the furnace pipes
about who had the most hits

Mother came down and broke-up
the fist fight, confiscating
our newly-cocked weapon
Took it upstairs and while
trying to unload it, pulled
the trigger, firing a bb
through the front room window
killing a robin in the hedge

We waited under the stairs
thinking about the tiny round hole
the long jagged crack in the view
of North Shore mountains
until the old man came home from work
Bury that damn bird, is all he said
We did, in a shoe box under the plum tree

Tim's Handshake

There is a method in telling every story
Some things about people are so uncertain
Posture, the way they move in the dark
The unusual scenarios they think about
in the early hours of the morning
Can you tell I'm being sincere when I say
every tick of the clock is pushing us closer to the edge
until there is nothing but acres of open water
or miles of sky falling beneath our feet

The day came when all things were perfectly balanced
The sun was at the correct angle
Gentle breezes rippled over deep green water
Flowers were smiling like lepers in the grass
The veiled insect bride in the tight sheath
struggled down the wedding bower
Nearby, asses in a field of clover
bray a solemn greeting or a song of pity
sadder than a worthless handshake

Liar's Club

Always listened to old men telling stories
How they paused and looked around the room
before finishing the spit
Didn't know what to believe
I thought they were all telling the truth
Now I know they were often telling lies
about the people who lived in them
during the hard times so long ago

Trips were longer, loads were bigger
the weather was colder and the women,
all gone now, were more beautiful than ever
You could eat for a week and get change from a dime
Cows gave cream, Angels worked in hospitals
Mothers were sacred, Fathers unremitting
Everybody was happier being poor

They remember friends lost in the war
Still young in their minds, like characters
from old heroic movies, who never age
If you want a cheerful song they know
all the words, verses and tunes
And cheat like hell at cards
Talking about when trains arrived on time
and bars provided free lunches

When they paused to say, *So help me God,*
lifting their ancient eyes to the ceiling
I would shudder inside knowing
I was about to hear something so remarkable
my ears might not survive the shock
It was always about the day they gave up drinking
or the honourable way they treated a woman

The Writer's Memoirs

There was nothing I could remember about any of my literary friends that was worth printing. The gossip I suppose would be of interest to themselves. Numerology of vowels and consonants making changeable relentless mythology. A weather forecast would be more reliable. Of my adult life, let it be said: hell on earth was a basket of acidic fruit. Blue with the marks of time. I saw a baby like that outside a K-Mart store. Dressed in filthy clothing, wearing a mouse under his eye. The father, one of those pinched faces that begat bruises. Discoloured, begging forehead. A cruel unhealing mouth. I still feel the shudder of violence that child wore under his soiled Barney Rubble t-shirt. The marks in a basket of rotting fruit are not so clearly read.

The Shallow Cupboard

House groaning all night
like an convulsing body
in its decrepit season
It finds mercy in every dawning
I woke up startled by a dream
Stars peering through the roof
into a house with empty cupboards
dirty tattered wallpaper

Outside the bedroom window
the swift sound of a bird
ripped from its branch
by talons in a feather pillow
The two hundred pound mastiff
wandering in the hall sniffs at my door knob
If I had one, I'd give him a cigar
or the knee bones of a big animal

By first light the bats in the attic
are making soft kissing noises
In bat speak it might be screaming
or tender echoes of bat copulation
Their kisses soothe the baby
already awake in her crib
She kisses back herself to sleep

Night Traveler

Tonight the wind scratches the house
brushing against climbing rose bushes
The cat paws at some invisible thing
I can't see, but it sees
sitting straight up watching flight
around the edges of the room
across a wall paper sky

Made me wonder if ghosts enjoy
watching people make love
maybe that's why they hang around
Standing naked in the hallway
I watched a man combing his hair
in front of the bathroom mirror
When I turned on the light he disappeared

Stayed awake the rest of the night
drinking coffee, writing a poem
about Rene Char and invisible handwriting
Time lost to a dripping tap
This is what the night would say
pushing the moon further into the darkness

Lake of the Moon

—for Dolores

Moon below us moving
through the hills
brightness turning gold
back into dust

full moonlight
in the coulees
the wooden match I lit
in the sheltering of your coat
went off like a gunshot

on this hill
a little above flatlands
in moonlight circumstances
your embracing arms
held my bones together

I gave you stone
you gave me body of earth
coyotes yapping in the wind
small trees making big
shadowy lunar pictures

Final Instructions

Burn this man
in a plain cardboard box
with a label that says;
This side up

Don't leave him too long
with the undertaker

Scatter the ashes
in a friendly place
where birds sing
and children play

The selected poems in this volume were taken from the following books:

The Naked Machine Rides On
God Loves Us Like Earthworms Love Wood
Advertisements For Paradise
On The Way To Ethiopia
All Night Highway